AN INTRODUCTION TO CULZEAN CASTLE

PRESENT-DAY VISITORS TO CULZEAN ARE ENCHANTED BY THE APPROACH TO THE CASTLE AS, FROM THE TOP OF THE HILL WITH ITS SUPERB PANORAMIC VIEW OVER THE FIRTH OF CLYDE, THE DRIVE WINDS THROUGH WOODED COUNTRYSIDE TOWARDS THE RUINED ARCH AND VIADUCT WHICH LEADS TO THE FRONT DOOR. ONE CAN ONLY MARVEL AT ITS TRULY SPECTACULAR SETTING, PERCHED ON A ROCKY PROMONTORY, OVERLOOKING THE SEA. TO MEDIEVAL EYES, HOWEVER, IN A SCOTLAND RIVEN WITH FEROCIOUS AND BLOODY FAMILY FEUDS, THE VERY QUALITIES THAT MAKE CULZEAN A SCENIC DELIGHT ARE THE ONES THAT MADE THIS SITE IMPORTANT TACTICALLY. PROTECTED BY TALL CLIFFS AND THE SEA ON ONE SIDE AND A STEEP GLEN ON THE OTHER, ANY HOUSE BUILT HERE WAS A FORTRESS.

Culzean from the north by
Alexander Nasmyth. THIS PAINTING
HANGS IN THE LONG DRAWING ROOM.

The first written references to a tower house at Culzean date to the 1400s although it is possible there was a building here even earlier. Then it was known as Coif Castle or the House of Cove, taking its name from the caves below. This was altered to Cullean Castle in the 1600s and the present spelling adopted sometime in the eighteenth century.

The recorded history of Culzean properly starts in 1569 when Sir Thomas Kennedy was given the Culzean estates by his brother, the 4th Earl of Cassillis. He began building or enlarging the tower house around the 1590s. An account of 1632 describes 'THE HOUSSE OF THE COVE buildid with grate cost and expensse, some 40 zeirs agoe by Sir Thomas Kennedy of Culzeane, Tutor of Cassiles'.

As times became settled, Culzean became more of a family home. By the seventeenth century terraces and pleasure gardens had been constructed. Since even then Culzean was rarely lived in all year round, improvements to the house were haphazard.

In the eighteenth century a chain of events occurred that transformed Culzean Castle from a relatively modest tower house into a neoclassical mansion. It was not so much a sudden influx of real wealth or real power that brought about this transformation but, rather, the desire to create a trophy house, a building that said, even shouted, that the Kennedy family had arrived.

What you see at Culzean Castle today is a result of many years of careful restoration by the National Trust for Scotland that has united the different stages of Culzean's aesthetic history. It reflects the different stages of Culzean's past, from Robert Adam's additions to the medieval tower house to its heyday as one of the grandest houses in Scotland.

Culzean from the south-east, seen through the Ruined Arch.

Culzean from the west.

Culzean from the south-west.

From 1973 until 1983 the National Trust for Scotland focused on the Adam elements of Culzean to the exclusion of the contribution made by successive members of the Kennedy family. In recent years there have been considerable advances in the Trust's knowledge of Adam's achievements thanks to new publications, notably Eileen Harris's *The Genius of Robert Adam; His Interiors* (2001). Professor Michael Moss's research, embodied in his *The Magnificent Castle of Culzean and the Kennedy Family* (2002) revealed the broader history of the house. It particularly clarified the pioneering Adam Revival work by the 3rd Marquess and his first wife and the contribution made by his second wife to recreating an eighteenth-century ethos in Culzean's major rooms.

Building on this knowledge, a new Master Plan for the castle and its collections was implemented in 2003. Its aim is to reflect how Culzean, like all great houses, has evolved over the centuries, according to changing tastes and fashions.

THE KENNEDY FAMILY

JOHN KENNEDY OF DUNURE
D. c1385

SIR GILBERT KENNEDY OF DUNURE
D. c1410

JAMES
D. 1408

SIR JOHN
D. c1435

LORD GILBERT
D. c1479

LORD JOHN
D. c1509

DAVID, 1ST EARL OF CASSILLIS
D. 1513

GILBERT, 2ND EARL OF CASSILLIS
D. 1527

GILBERT, 3RD EARL
1515-1558

GILBERT, 4TH EARL
c1543-1576

SIR THOMAS OF CULZEAN 'THE TUTOR'
1548/9-1602

JOHN, 5TH EARL
c1574-1615

HEW, MASTER OF CASSILLIS
D. BEFORE 1607

THOMAS
D. 1601

JAMES OF CULZEAN
afterwards BLAIRQUHAN

SIR ALEXANDER OF CRAIGOCH
later CULZEAN c1585-1652

JOHN, 6TH EARL
c1598-1668

JOHN OF CULZEAN
c1620-1665

**ALEXANDER OF CRAIGOCH
AND KILHENZIE** c1625-1698

JOHN, 7TH EARL
c1640-1701

SIR ARCHIBALD THE WICKED OF CULZEAN
c1655-1710

ARCHIBALD OF NEW YORK
c1685-1763

JOHN, LORD KENNEDY
1670-1700

SIR JOHN OF CULZEAN
c1680-1742

JOHN, 8TH EARL
1700-1759

SIR JOHN
1720-1744

SIR THOMAS, 9TH EARL
1726-1775

SIR DAVID, 10TH EARL
1727-1792

ARCHIBALD, CAPT. RN 11TH EARL
1718-1794

The Culzean Kennedys are one of Scotland's oldest families and trace their ancestry to Robert the Bruce. A descendant of his, John Kennedy of Dunure, acquired Cassillis Castle in Ayrshire and other land in Ayrshire and Wigtownshire around 1350.

In 1458 Sir Gilbert Kennedy was made Lord Kennedy. His grandson was created the first Earl of Cassillis in 1510.

Sir Thomas of Culzean 'The Tutor of Cassillis'.

Sir Thomas was taken prisoner at the Battle of Langside fighting for the cause of Mary, Queen of Scots and was later rewarded with a knighthood for his loyalty by her son, James VI and I. He was granted the lands of Culzean, an area that stretched from Ayr to Girvan and inland to Loch Doon, and was known as the Tutor of Cassillis because he was guardian to his nephew, the 5th Earl. Later he played a leading role in a bitter feud between the senior Kennedys and the Kennedys of Bargany, a junior branch of the family. It began with a disputed inheritance but soon progressed into all-out war and resulted in the deaths of both Kennedy of Bargany and Sir Thomas, who was ambushed and murdered as he rode from Greenan Castle to Ayr, in 1602.

The 4th Earl of Cassillis in his stronghold of Castle Kennedy was so powerful that he was known as the King of Carrick. He and his brother Sir Thomas became infamous throughout Scotland for their cruel treatment of the Abbot of Crossraguel Abbey whom they roasted in an effort to gain possession of the Abbey lands.

Sir Thomas Kennedy's heir, his son James, sold the Culzean estate to another brother, Alexander Kennedy, whose son is the direct ancestor of the present Marquess of Ailsa.

This family tree is not comprehensive and does not necessarily include all the children of a marriage.

FAR LEFT
John,
7th Earl of Cassillis.

LEFT
Thomas,
9th Earl of Cassillis.

FAR LEFT
David,
10th Earl of Cassillis.

LEFT
Archibald,
11th Earl of Cassillis.

Jean, the sister of the 4th Earl and Sir Thomas Kennedy, had the sad task of tying the scarf around Mary, Queen of Scots' eyes before her execution for treason by her cousin, Queen Elizabeth I of England, in 1587. The Kennedy family still have Mary's crucifix and other tokens of affection given to Lady Jean that morning.

Sir Archibald Kennedy fought for the cause of Catholic Stuart King James II who was replaced on the throne by Protestant William of Orange in 1688. Because of his Jacobite sympathies, Sir Archibald, at one time, hid in the caves beneath Culzean to avoid being imprisoned for treason.

In 1759, John Kennedy, the 8th Earl of Cassillis died. And here, from the point of view of Culzean and the Kennedys, is where it all gets interesting. Why? Because now the Earldom of Cassillis and the ownership of Culzean were reunited in the person of Sir Thomas Kennedy for the first time since the 4th Earl had given Culzean to his brother in 1569. Sir Thomas inherited Culzean from his older brother in 1744, and the Earldom and estates of Cassillis from his kinsman, the 8th Earl, fifteen years later. He was challenged by a rival heir, William Douglas, later the Duke of Queensberry, who claimed descent on the female line. Three years later the House of Lords settled the dispute in favour of Sir Thomas Kennedy who was confirmed 9th Earl of Cassillis. Now the story of Culzean Castle as it is today begins.

THE AILSA EXHIBITION

The Ailsa Room, on the ground floor of the Castle presents highlights of the history of the Culzean Kennedys.

1387	Geoffrey Chaucer begins work on *The Canterbury Tales*.
1388	Border warfare results in victory for the Scots at Otterburn.
1390	Robert III becomes King of Scotland.
1412	First Scottish university created at St Andrews.
1415	The English defeat the French at Agincourt.
1455	Beginning of the War of the Roses, civil war between the royal houses of York and Lancaster.
1485	Battle of Bosworth Field, Henry Tudor defeats Richard III to become Henry VII.
1503	Margaret, daughter of Henry VII, marries James IV of Scotland.
1513	Battle of Flodden, James IV of Scotland killed in battle where the English defeat the Scots.
1558	Elizabeth I, daughter of Henry VIII and Anne Boleyn, becomes Queen of England.
1560	Treaty of Berwick and Treaty of Edinburgh between England and Scotland, resulted in the ending of the Auld Alliance between Scotland and France.
1567	Murder of Lord Darnley, husband of Mary, Queen of Scots, probably murdered by Bothwell. Mary then marries Bothwell, is imprisoned and then forced to abdicate. Her son James VI becomes King of Scotland.
1569	*Sir Thomas Kennedy, granted the lands of Culzean by his brother Gilbert, 4th Earl of Cassillis.*
1587	Mary, Queen of Scots executed for treason.
1588	Spanish Armada defeated by English navy.
1602	*Sir Thomas Kennedy murdered.*
1603	Elizabeth I dies and James VI of Scotland becomes James I of England.
1605	Gunpowder Plot – Guy Fawkes and other Roman Catholics attempt to blow up Parliament and James I.
1622	*James Kennedy, heir of Sir Thomas sold Culzean to his brother Alexander Kennedy of Craigoch.*
1625	Charles I becomes King of England.
1642	English Civil War breaks out between Royalists and Parliamentarians.
1645	Charles I defeated at Battle of Naseby.
1649	Charles I executed.
1650	Charles II lands in Scotland and proclaimed King.
1651	Scotland invades England and is defeated at Battle of Worcester.
1660	Convention Parliament restores Charles II to throne.
1685	James VII of Scotland and James II of England is crowned.
1688	'Glorious Revolution' – William of Orange is invited to save England from Roman Catholicism, lands in England and James II flees to France.
1689	Battle of Killiecrankie – Jacobites beat Williamite forces, although later broken and beaten at Dunkeld.
1692	Glencoe Massacre.
1698	Darien Venture – Scottish attempts at creating a colony in Central America end in disaster, nearly bankrupting Scotland.
1707	Act of Union unites the parliaments of Scotland and England and transfers the seat of Scottish Government to London.
1714	Hanoverian George I becomes King.
1715	Jacobite Rebellion, aim to replace George with the 'Old Pretender', James VII and II's son. Defeated at Battle of Sheriffmuir.
1745	Jacobite Rebellion in Scotland led by 'Bonnie Prince Charlie' defeats Government forces at Prestonpans and advances into England.
1746	Jacobites crushed by Duke of Cumberland at Culloden.

Sir Thomas Kennedy by William Mosman, 1746. In this portrait he is holding a book by Vauban, the famous French military engineer.
THIS PORTRAIT HANGS IN THE BLUE DRAWING ROOM.

THOMAS KENNEDY
9TH EARL OF CASSILLIS
The Improving Earl

THOMAS KENNEDY WAS THE SECOND OF the three brothers to inherit Culzean in the eighteenth century and the first of the Culzean Kennedys to embark on large scale improvements to the Castle and estates.

In 1742, when his brother John inherited Culzean, Thomas Kennedy had already decided on a career in the army and, in 1744, bought a commission in the 33rd Regiment of Footguards and went to fight in Flanders. Whilst there he learned that John had died. He was now Sir Thomas Kennedy of Culzean.

Shortly after his coming of age, Sir Thomas returned to Ayrshire to attend to affairs at Culzean. Much needed to be done as the estate and the house had been greatly neglected. As a first step, Sir Thomas instituted an extensive programme of land improvements (see page 58 for more about the Culzean estates).

Section of the plan for Culzean estate in 1775 by John Foulis. It shows the walled garden beneath the castle and the Cow Park, which later became the Swan Pond.

Elevation for a 'casine' designed by William Chambers in 1759 for Sir Thomas, but never built.

Whilst all this was underway Sir Thomas travelled on the Continent on the fashionable Grand Tour (see page 15). In Rome he acquired the beginnings of his art collection including works by Piranesi, old master paintings and prints and classical statues. His exposure to classical art and architecture also inspired him with ideas on how to improve his run-down house.

A few of the works of art purchased by the 9th Earl, photographed by the 3rd Marquess in the 1880s.

It was the convention for aristocratic cultural pilgrims to have their portraits painted in the eternal city. Batoni was one of the most sought-after artists. This painting was long thought to portray Earl David, the 9th Earl's younger brother. Recent research has confirmed it to be Thomas Kennedy, revealing the work to be the only known survivor at Culzean of the art collection acquired by the 9th Earl during his Grand Tour.

THIS PORTRAIT HANGS IN THE LIBRARY

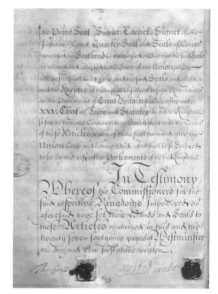

Articles of Union between England and Scotland from the House of Lords record office, 1707.

In 1759 the 8th Earl of Cassillis died having left the whole of the Cassillis estate to Sir Thomas. Three years later Sir Thomas was declared 9th Earl of Cassillis.

He had already begun modernising the Castle and, in 1750, had created a new dining room on the ground floor with views out to the garden terraces (now the Library). Later, the roofs and turrets were rebuilt and the walls of the tower house heightened to allow for the remodelling of the top floor. The Earl also commissioned a two-storey slant block facing out to the sea. Known as the 'office houses of Culzean' it contained the estate offices, a new billiard room and other rooms (see diagram on page 17).

In 1774 Earl Thomas was elected a Representative Peer of Scotland. He did not live long to enjoy this honour as he became ill in the summer of 1775 and died in Edinburgh later that year.

House of Lords from Ackermann's *Microcosm of London* by T. Rowlandson & A.C. Pugin.

After the 1707 Act of Union joined the English and Scottish Parliaments, the system of Representative Peers was introduced. Scottish hereditary peers had no automatic right to sit in the House of Lords at Westminster. Instead, twelve Scottish Representative Peers were elected by their fellow peers to seats in the Lords for a period of five years at a time. It was an important and prestigious office.

Illegal Gains

SMUGGLING AT CULZEAN

The Firth of Clyde was a notorious centre for smuggling and the fortified caves beneath Culzean were ideal for hiding contraband from the Revenue officers. For centuries the Culzean Kennedys and others on the estate were either directly involved in smuggling or turned a blind eye to it, in exchange for a share of the profits.

One reason why smuggling, or 'the Running Trade', was so widespread on the Ayrshire coast was because of its proximity to the Isle of Man. Smuggling was a major activity on the island because goods could be legally imported on payment of small duties to the Lord of Man and then shipped into England, Scotland and Ireland, where they were either forbidden or attracted high duties.

CULZEAN CASTLE

ISLE OF MAN

Culzean by Moonlight by Alexander Nasmyth: smugglers can be seen in the foreground unloading contraband.

The exterior and interior of the caves on the foreshore of Culzean.

Records at Culzean show an Archibald Kennedy (no direct relation), the estate factor in 1747, conducting a thriving business from the Castle in partnership with George Moore, one of the most famous and successful of the Manx smugglers, and Sir Thomas Kennedy, later 9th Earl of Cassillis. They traded in Lisbon (port), claret, rum, spirits and Congo tea which they smuggled in from the Isle of Man and sold locally. Earl Thomas was an ardent Jacobite and supported the return of the Stuart dynasty, the 'kings over the water', as did most of his Ayrshire smuggling network. Their activities were not only highly profitable but also a way of expressing their defiance of the Hanoverian government.

In the 1760s smuggling activities at Culzean were seriously curtailed by the increased vigilance of the Revenue officers. It would not do for a peer of the realm to be caught breaking the law so Earl Thomas diversified into the slave trade, an activity that also significantly increased the income of the estate.

David Kennedy, 10th Earl of Cassillis.

DAVID KENNEDY

10TH EARL OF CASSILLIS

The Builder Earl

DAVID KENNEDY, THE 10TH EARL OF CASSILLIS, was an enthusiastic and knowledgeable patron of architecture who succeeded in transforming Culzean Castle into an elegant, fashionable country seat.

James Boswell
by Sir Joshua Reynolds, 1785.

His social position meant that Earl David was considered to be very good husband material but he showed little interest in getting married. In 1782, his friend James Boswell composed a teasing song about him:

The Coopers they came to Lord Cassillis at Colzean
With their hoops all tight and ready
From London they came down
baith the black and the brown
And they wanted to give him a lady

Your Lordship, we pray, may not say us nae
For it's now full time you was girded [married]
Quoth the Earl 'Faith my dears, so great are my fears
In conscience I'd rather be yearded [buried]'.

The Coopers refer to the daughters of Sir Grey Cooper, a political ally of the Earl. David Kennedy was most definitely not amused but eventually forgave Boswell and their friendship was restored.

David Kennedy was born in 1727, the eighteenth of a family of twenty children, of whom only seven survived into adulthood. He became a barrister and practised on the Scottish circuit until 1768, when he was elected MP for the County of Ayr.

In 1775 David's life changed dramatically when his brother died. By all accounts he was particularly close to Thomas and would have been deeply upset by his death. But now the title and the estates of Culzean and Cassillis were his. In 1776, Earl David too was elected a Representative Peer. Almost immediately he began to transform his boyhood home into a house worthy of his new status. His thoughts turned to the most fashionable architect of the day and that year he invited Robert Adam to Culzean to draw up plans for rebuilding the Castle.

Although they were the largest landowners in Ayrshire, the Earls of Cassillis were by no means the richest. Much of their land was poor hill land and the family had few sources of income other than from the estates. Aristocrats who wanted to improve their finances often married heiresses but this was a path that David Kennedy resisted. Like his brother, he remained unmarried. Which raises the question of why he needed a house like Culzean, particularly as his own house was close by and easily large enough for a bachelor. One explanation is that he saw the rebuilding of the ancestral Kennedy home as an affirmation of the importance of the Culzean Kennedys and their hereditary right to the disputed Earldom of Cassillis.

Earl David continued to improve the estate at the same time that the Castle was being rebuilt. He commissioned Robert Adam to design several other buildings at Culzean including the Viaduct, the Ruined Arch and a new Home Farm. Despite the expense and the upheaval he seems to have remained cheerful. Indeed his jovial nature was noted by contemporaries, including James Boswell, the biographer of the famous Dr Johnson, who described him as a 'joker ... and nothing more ... a good honest merry fellow indeed ...'. However, in late 1790, burdened by illness and increasing debt, he wrote morosely instructing his banker to hand over more money for the work at Culzean: 'I hope my operations will soon be at an end as I am really wearied of Building and wish to be at rest.' Two years later he died, leaving debts of £60,000 (over £4 million in today's money) most of which he had incurred in the rebuilding of Culzean Castle and the improvement of his estates.

Infant mortality rates were very high in the early years of the eighteenth century. In fact half of all deaths in Scotland were children under the age of ten. To lose thirteen children, as the Kennedys did, was not that unusual. They were possibly carried off by diseases that are considered minor nowadays. In those days, without antibiotics and expert medical care, even the common cold could be fatal.

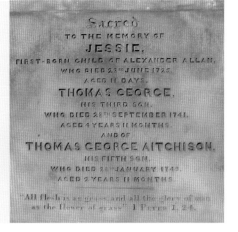

Robert Adam
attributed to George Willison
circa 1770-1775.

ROBERT ADAM
The Master Architect

ROBERT ADAM WAS POSSIBLY THE MOST IMPORTANT British architect of the late eighteenth century, equally well known as a decorator and furniture designer. The synthesis of architecture, planning and decoration into an integrated whole is the hallmark of his unique style.

A Robert Adam drawing of the exterior wall at Emperor Diocletian's ruined palace in Spalatro (now Split in Croatia).

Charlotte Square in Edinburgh's New Town was Robert Adam's last commission and is considered to be one of the finest urban spaces in Europe.

Robert Adam was born in Fife in 1728 and moved to Edinburgh at the age of eleven. His father, William Adam, was Scotland's foremost architect, with a thriving practice and an established reputation. When he died in 1748, Robert's older brother John took over his practice and Robert joined him.

In 1754 Robert went to Europe on the Grand Tour as part of his master plan to find inspiration in classical architecture in order to be able to develop his own style and work on a grander scale. What he learned during these years he was to draw on for the rest of his life.

In 1758 he moved to London in pursuit of the opportunities that existed in the elegant and moneyed south. He was joined first by his brother, James, and later by another brother, William.

The Adams soon became immensely successful. There was a mania for the 'beautiful spirit of antiquity' amongst men of taste and Robert was considered an expert on classical architecture. He knew he had to create something new to attract the wealthy, aristocratic patrons he sought. He developed a distinctive style that was based on the classical forms he had studied in Italy and in Split but with elements of Greek, Gothic and even Egyptian architecture. When he was given the opportunity, he designed every detail of an interior including the furniture, carpets and fittings to ensure that the whole conformed to his aesthetic ideal. Over the years he built a trusted team of artists and craftsmen who could work to his high standards, particularly on the finer details such as delicate plasterwork and painting.

The Library at Syon House by Robert Adam, built between 1760-69.

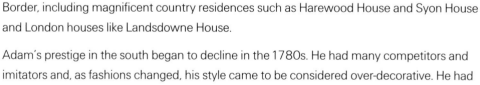

Culzean Castle from the north
by Robert Adam, 1784.

Culzean Castle from the south
by Robert Adam.

Between 1758 and 1779 Robert and James Adam worked on 147 projects south of the Border, including magnificent country residences such as Harewood House and Syon House and London houses like Landsdowne House.

Adam's prestige in the south began to decline in the 1780s. He had many competitors and imitators and, as fashions changed, his style came to be considered over-decorative. He had also experienced financial difficulties due of the failure of his London property development venture. By the time he was involved in building Culzean, most of his commissions were in Scotland. By now his thinking had moved on from richly ornamented classicism to a simpler, more dramatic castle style which drew on traditional Scottish, Ancient Roman, medieval and Renaissance architecture.

Culzean, with its massing of crenellated wings, square turrets, battlements and central monumental rotunda perched on a rocky promontory, is the very essence of Adam's romantic vision. Its interiors, although plain to English eyes, were lavish by Scottish standards.

Robert Adam never saw Culzean completed. He died in 1792 at his home in London from a stomach condition brought on, it is said, by overwork. He is buried in Westminster Abbey, a fitting tribute to one who was the greatest architect and designer of his day.

The Grand Tour

AN OPEN UNIVERSITY

In this painting Sir Thomas Kennedy of Culzean, later the 9th Earl of Cassillis, is on the left, playing his bass viol (similar to a cello), with his friends Lord Charlemont, Lord Midleton, Lord Bruce, the Hon John Ward and other members of his set in Rome.

Sir Thomas was part of a circle of young aristocrats who embarked on the fashionable Grand Tour, travelling on the Continent for a number of years to visit the sites most associated with classical art and architecture. These cultural pilgrimages were an essential element of the education of the British upper classes and formed aristocratic taste for generations to come. The young milords were passionately interested in art and the antique. They visited galleries and churches and became obsessive collectors of Greek and Roman statues and old master paintings. When they returned, they often began decorating their homes in the classical style.

Parody of the School of Athens by Sir Joshua Reynolds, 1751. It depicts Sir Thomas Kennedy playing the bass viol, similar to a cello, in the group on the left.

Robert Adam's experience was slightly different. When he set off on his Grand Tour, he first travelled as part of Lord Charles Hope's entourage of rich and titled friends. Their lifestyle was well beyond his means, however, and he was going abroad to improve his career prospects. He lived in Rome for two years where he studied under Piranesi, the famous antiquarian, and the French draughtsman, Charles-Louis Clérisseau, both of whom he greatly admired. He drew and recorded buildings and classical ruins, and spent five weeks at Emperor Diocletian's ruined palace in Spalatro (now Split in Croatia), publishing a portfolio of drawings which was to further enhance his reputation.

REBUILDING OF CULZEAN

WHEN EARL DAVID COMMISSIONED Robert Adam to rebuild Culzean in the 1770s the house consisted of the original four-storey tower with a collection of offices to the north-east and a separate two-storey wing extending westwards along the cliff edge. Over fifteen years and in several stages this hotchpotch was transformed into an elegant, fashionable home.

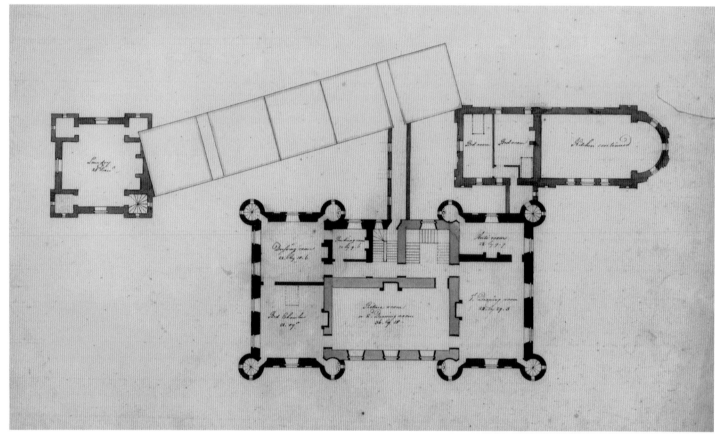

Robert Adam's proposal for the first floor (first stage, 1777), showing the L-shaped tower house squared up and the wings added. The kitchen was built onto the 1760s block but the laundry was never built.

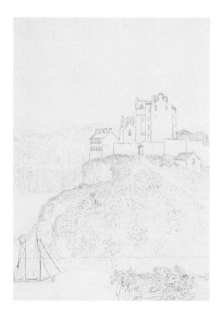

The first stage of Adam's rebuilding of Culzean in the 1770s was the squaring-up of the 'L' of the sixteenth-century tower house, with the addition of a wing on either side to form a rectangular house with turrets at each corner. A new kitchen block was also constructed at this time and, in 1779, a round brewhouse, a milkhouse, bath-house and further bedrooms were added.

By 1784 Earl David had decided he wanted a sea outlook from the Castle. Adam produced a design for a new north-facing front — a three-storey drum tower with a circular saloon with rooms on either side on the very edge of the cliffs looking out to sea. It was an ambitious scheme that would double the size of the castle and require the demolition of the 9th Earl's wing. In 1787 this dramatic design was refined further to include a top-lit oval staircase to replace the existing front and back stairs. The main house, finished only six years earlier, would have to have the entire centre of its front removed. The scheme was extremely costly and would involve enormous upheaval but, to Earl David's great credit, he accepted Adam's proposals.

Culzean from the west sketched prior to Robert Adam's design in 1776.

Culzean from the south-east attributed to Robert Adam, after the first stage of Adam's alterations.
THIS PAINTING HANGS IN THE EISENHOWER APARTMENT.

By late 1790 building work on the second stage of Culzean was well under way. Despite the expense Earl David was determined that it should be finished to Adam's designs. A letter from Robert Adam's brother-in-law at this time refers to 'the whimsical but magnificent Castle of Colane ... on which the Earl ... encouraged him to indulge to the utmost his romantic genius ...'

Robert Adam's proposal for the second floor (second stage, 1779), showing the brewhouse block with the 1760s wing still in place.

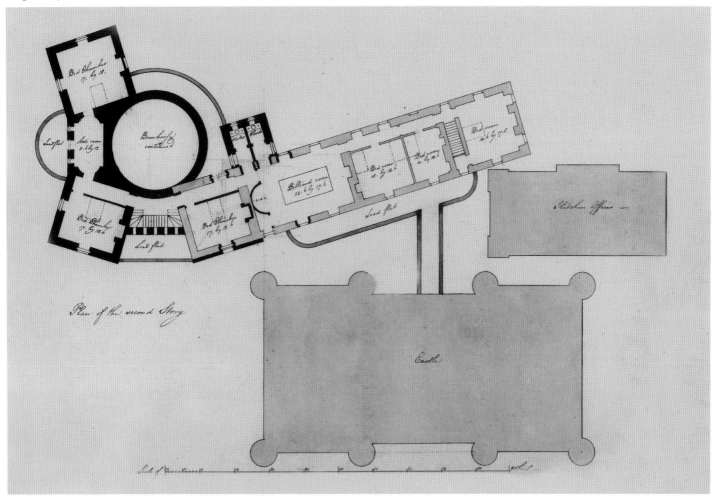

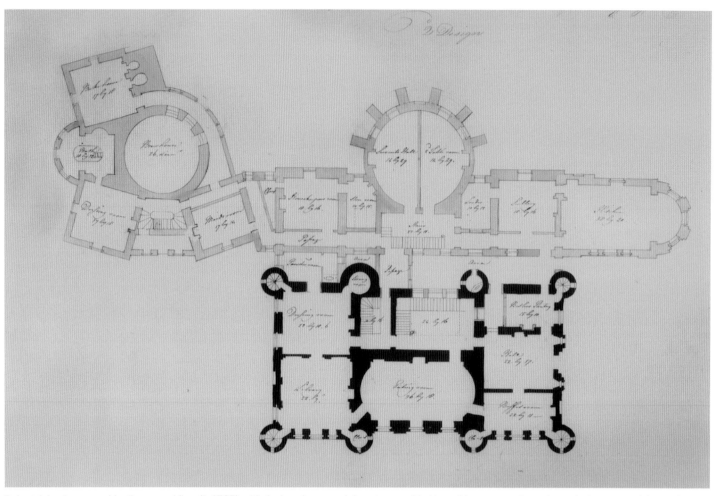

Robert Adam's proposal for the ground floor (in 1785), with the brewhouse and drum tower added but with a rectangular staircase in the centre of the castle.

Robert Adam's proposals for the first floor (final stage, 1787), showing the Oval Staircase and the Round Drawing Room, called the Saloon by Robert Adam.

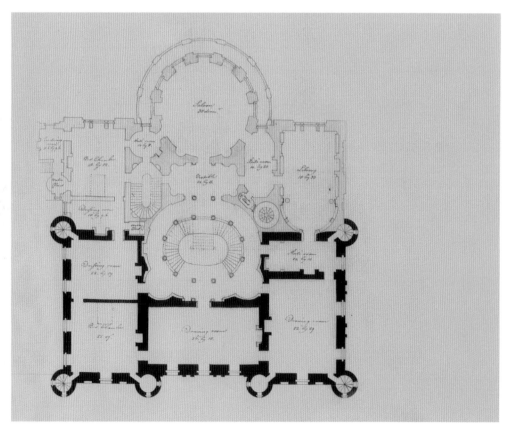

Robert Adam's proposal for the east elevation.

Earl David continued to spend vast amounts of money not just on construction work but on decoration, fittings and furniture for the castle until the estate was virtually bankrupt. Records show that, between 1788 and 1790, more than £5,000 (the equivalent of £300,000 today) was paid for demolition and quarrying works alone. Between 1787 and 1792 accounts sent to the Earl by Hugh Cairncross amounted to over £7,000 for work done at the house and on the other Adam buildings at Culzean. A conservative guess therefore is that two or three million pounds in today's money went into the creation of Robert Adam's Culzean.

The main building materials used at Culzean were obtained locally. The sandstone, for example, came from Blanefield Quarry by Kirkoswald, about seven miles away. Many items were brought to Culzean by sea because it was easier than carrying goods on the roads of the time.

The most elaborate elements such as the chimneypieces would be carved in a specialist workshop in London and taken to Culzean by sea or road. The stucco plasterwork was either cast in the workshop and then pinned to the ceilings or sometimes carved on site. Earl David was loyal to his workforce and a letter from Robert Adam of 1790 details his intention that the ornamental stucco for the Round Drawing Room and Staircase should be 'done by Mr Coney though he [the Earl] knew he was given to drinking, yet he did not like new people ...'

Archibald, Captain RN,
11th Earl of Cassillis
by Mather Brown, 1793.
The battle of the Tagus,
the naval action fought
by Captain Kennedy
off Lisbon, in April 1760,
is shown in the
background.
THIS PORTRAIT HANGS IN
THE DINING ROOM.

ARCHIBALD KENNEDY

11TH EARL OF CASSILLIS

The American Earl

IN 1783 EARL DAVID CHANGED THE TERMS of his brother's will to entail the estates of Culzean and Cassillis to a distant cousin, Captain Archibald Kennedy, a wealthy naval captain from New York. This was a crucial decision as, although it caused a legal dispute that tied up the estate for years, it handed over the title, estates, and his beautiful but incomplete house to someone who had the means to keep them intact. It could be argued that the influx of American money ultimately saved Culzean.

Born in what were then the American colonies in 1719, Archibald had joined the Royal Navy at an early age and saw action in numerous conflicts both in Europe and North America. Whilst on a tour of duty in America he married a wealthy heiress, Catherine Schuyler, and bought No.1 Broadway in New York, where he built a fine house.

HMS *Flamborough* in action against two French frigates in April 1760 in the battle of the Tagus.

Archibald went on to distinguish himself in the Seven Years War (1756-1763) when, as the commander of HMS *Flamborough*, his job was to protect British trade with Portugal. A major attraction of a posting such as this was the prize money to be earned through the capture of enemy ships. The captain could claim up to three-eighths of the value of an enemy ship, its cargo and a per capita fee for the number of prisoners taken. In Portuguese waters the pickings were rich and Archibald was so successful in capturing enemy vessels that he netted an estimated £200,000 in prize money. His gallantry was recognised by the grateful British community in Lisbon who, in 1760, presented him with a silver salver engraved with a scene of his most notable action.

The silver salver presented to Captain Kennedy in gratitude by the British community in Lisbon.

Southeast Prospect of the City of New York,
circa 1756-7 by unknown American artist,
showing Royal Navy ships at anchor.

In 1763 the war in Europe ended and Archibald Kennedy was sent back to the New York station.
Here he was the second most senior British officer in North America and played a key role in the
events that led up to the American War of Independence. After the death of his first wife
Catherine Schuyler, he married Anne Watts in 1769, the daughter of another wealthy New York
merchant, and extended his already substantial property empire. His house at No.1 Broadway
became the British headquarters when war broke out. He remained in America until 1781
when he took his young family to the safety of London. He returned to New York alone only to
find much of his property confiscated including his Broadway house, which had been taken over
by George Washington. He returned permanently to London where he was able to transform his
considerable wealth into an even bigger fortune through prudent investments.

In December 1792 Archibald Kennedy became the 11th Earl of Cassillis and the new owner
of Culzean. It was not entirely an occasion to rejoice since the estate was now bankrupt. There
was also a rival heir who pursued his claim doggedly through the courts until agreement was
finally reached many years later.

The by now elderly 11th Earl did not live long enough to enjoy Culzean. He visited in 1793 and
ordered fabrics, curtains, wallpaper and furniture for his new home. On the return journey to
England, his wife was taken ill in Edinburgh and died there. A year later, the 11th Earl died,
passing the title and estates to his eldest son, Archibald.

Troops escort the stamped paper
to city hall, New York 1765.

The Stamp Act was a tax-raising measure imposed by the British Government on the
American colonies, which required official revenue stamps to be attached to all printed
matter including newspapers and legal documents. It was deeply unpopular amongst the
colonists and, in 1765, led to riots and civil disturbance in Boston, New York and other
American cities. Captain Kennedy became embroiled in the Stamp Act crisis as the
commander of the Royal Navy ships in New York. First he successfully thwarted a plot to
destroy the stamps as they arrived in New York from Britain. He followed this up by refusing
to allow unstamped cargoes to leave port, an action that made him very unpopular amongst
New York's merchants. As a result of their misrepresentation of his motives Captain Kennedy
was formally accused of 'lack of zeal for His Majesty's service', relieved of his command and
sent back to London. He quickly convinced the Lords of the Admiralty that he was innocent
of any crime and returned to his post in triumph.

Anne Watts, second wife of the 11th Earl,
by Mather Brown, 1793.
THIS PORTRAIT HANGS IN THE DINING ROOM.

INHERITANCE LAW

It is almost impossible to understand the history of Scotland's great country houses without an elementary grasp of the complicated laws of entail. At its simplest the entail system was designed to ensure that wherever the title went, so too did the land and that they passed from one generation to the next. Since ownership of land was what made a family part of the aristocracy it had to be preserved at all costs. An entail in Scottish law was a legal agreement with statutory protection and its terms usually stipulated those parts of the estate that could never be sold or pass to other descendants apart from the designated heir. There were advantages too in that no part of an entailed estate could be confiscated for debt or non-payment of taxes, nor could an eldest son be disinherited on the whim of his father. Improvements made to an entailed estate could later be charged to the estate, not the individual 'heir in possession'.

By the 1790s the terms of the entail could be got around by obtaining a special Act of Parliament giving permission to sell land to repay debts if the heir agreed, as often happened at Culzean. From the 1840s, entails in Scotland could be terminated with the heir's consent by applying to the courts.

THE ENTRANCE AND ARMOURY

VISITORS ENTER THE CASTLE by the Porch, designed by Wardrop & Reid in 1877 to create an airlock buffering the interior from the strong sea breezes. On either side of the entrance are the rooms which the 3rd Marquess annexed for his boat-building business. The drawing office to the left contains bookcases, with their original arched recesses, rescued along with decorative ornaments and plaster figures from the original Adam Library. The collection of 'half-hulls' illustrate the form of the various yachts the 3rd Marquess built.

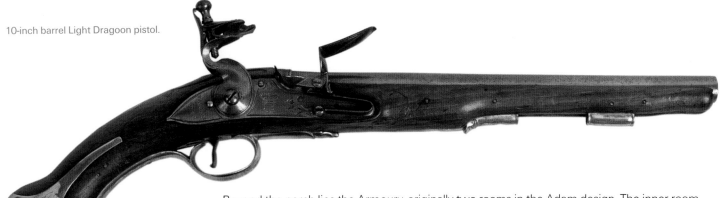

10-inch barrel Light Dragoon pistol.

Beyond the porch lies the Armoury, originally two rooms in the Adam design. The inner room, by the fireplace, was the Entrance Hall. The chimneypiece here was designed by Adam in 1778 and is executed in natural stone to complement the plain Doric frieze above. The smaller area south of the columns was the Buffet Room, leading from what was the Eating Room next door. All that survives of the Adam style of this area is the lozenge-patterned frieze over the door, an example of how, in almost all of Adam's early Culzean interiors, the door-friezes repeated the room cornices to create a unified effect.

Boasting around 24 different varieties of British Army flintlock pistol, the Armoury was established by the 12th Earl as part of his plan to complete the decoration of Culzean, which included finishing off the Oval Staircase and the Round Drawing Room. In 1812 he purchased from the Office of Ordnance at the Tower of London a number of obsolete weapons for display purposes. The wooden wall mountings were made by Adam & Robertson of Lambeth and sent to Culzean by sea, via the port of Leith. Once the frames were in place the weapons were sent along with one of the men from the Tower to 'fix them up in the proper manner'.

When the Armoury was expanded into two rooms, the weapons were rearranged to fill the enlarged space. The collection was also extended over the years: for example, the propeller on the ceiling is a memento of World War I, presented to the 3rd Marquess by No 1 Fighting School at Turnberry in 1919.

As it is now, the Armoury is home to one of the most important collections of arms in existence. It is the largest collection of these apart from Her Majesty the Queen's at Windsor Castle. It is particularly significant because all of the weapons have been used, many in the service of notable British regiments and the East India Company.

HANGER SWORDS

The latticed frame on the west wall is made up of 111 cut and shaped 'hanger' sword hilts. With their simple shell-hilts and knuckle-bows, hanger swords were the common, single edge swords normally issued to infantry troops. There are so many varieties of this weapon in the Tower of London and elsewhere that it is assumed that the Colonels of each regiment, who had to pay for their arms, favoured different designs. The 'private man', as soldiers of the seventeenth century were known, carried a sword as a 'last resort' weapon for close-quarters fighting. As muskets and bayonets became standard issue in the eighteenth century, the sword of the infantry private gradually ceased to exist as a fighting weapon although it remained an essential piece of equipment for parade and ceremonial occasions.

Major Charles Hamilton Wake, 34th Native Indian Infantry by Mary Ellen Best, 1842.

The 12th Earl of Cassillis and 1st Marquess of Ailsa by William Owen. The Earl is in his coronation robes and the background echoes the colonnaded splendour of the Oval Staircase in a more ornamental form.

THIS PORTRAIT HANGS IN THE OVAL STAIRCASE.

ARCHIBALD KENNEDY

12TH EARL OF CASSILLIS
1ST MARQUESS OF AILSA

The Ambitious Earl

Marchioness of Ailsa, formerly Margaret
Erskine of Dun, by William Owen.
This portrait is the companion piece to
the portrait of her husband, opposite.
THIS PORTRAIT HANGS IN THE OVAL STAIRCASE.

BLESSED WITH YOUTH AND THE FORTUNE he had inherited from his father Archibald
Kennedy, the 12th Earl had the energy and resources to bring Robert Adam's vision for
Culzean to fruition.

The 12th Earl was born in America in 1770. He married Margaret Erskine in 1793. She was
the daughter of John Erskine of Dun, a wealthy landowner who left his estates to her second
son, John, who took the name Kennedy Erskine.

William IV by Henry Edward Dawe, *circa* 1830.

The 12th Earl was extremely ambitious. He wanted to be made a Representative Peer of Scotland and a British Peer who, unlike the holder of a Scottish peerage, could have a permanent seat in the House of Lords and hence the possibility of a great office of state. In pursuit of these goals he continued to pester anyone of importance who crossed his path. Unfortunately his habit of changing political sides made him as many enemies as friends. He often used Culzean in his quest for advancement. Hearing that Sir Robert Peel, the then Prime Minister, was to holiday in Scotland he instantly wrote to offer hospitality. Earlier Lord Melville, the most important figure in Scottish politics, had been a guest at Culzean.

In 1806 his efforts began to pay off and the 12th Earl was made Baron Ailsa, taking his title from Ailsa Craig, the plug of volcanic rock in the Firth of Clyde just south-west of the Castle. But it was his friendship with the Duke of Clarence, later to become King William IV, that was to be his greatest asset. They had met as boys in America and their two families continued to be close. In 1827 the Earl's son, John Kennedy Erskine, married Augusta Fitzclarence, the illegitimate daughter of the Duke and Mrs Jordan. In 1831, when William became King, Archibald was made 1st Marquess of Ailsa.

For aristocrats the country seat was both a showcase and a playground. The 1st Marquess spent large sums on the Castle and its grounds, and the family usually spent the summer months there and winters at their London home for 'the Season'.

The Earl of Cassillis's London town house in Privy Gardens, looking east, by Alexander Nasmyth. Lady Cassillis and two of her children are on the terrace in the foreground.

The Port of Leith by Paul Jean Clays.

The 12th Earl of Cassillis, later the 1st Marquess of Ailsa (1770-1846) by Benjamin Marshall. The Earl is on his horse, Chancellor, winner of the first Ayr Gold Cup. The 12th Earl was a fine horseman who had begun training horses at Culzean in the 1790s. He was one of the founders of the Ayr Gold Cup held annually for horses trained in Scotland.

THIS PORTRAIT NOW HANGS IN THE DINING ROOM.

London was the centre of high society and its calendar was ruled by parliamentary sittings and the need to be close to court and political circles.

The journeys of aristocratic families between their various homes were often like full-scale house removals, transporting furniture, paintings, silver, linen, and crockery. Improvements in the design of carriages and better roads meant that travelling was not as difficult as it had been even fifty years before when packhorses and sledges were used in Ayrshire because of poor roads. From Culzean the family travelled to Leith, near Edinburgh, in a large state coach, escorted by armed outriders in livery, with the servants following in an ordinary coach. Here they took a ship for London whilst the grooms and coaches travelled on by road. Life got even more complicated in 1812 when the death of his father-in-law meant that the 12th Earl became responsible for the affairs of the House of Dun in Montrose, now owned by the National Trust for Scotland, which then became a destination on the annual migrations.

The 1st Marquess was a man of many interests. He was a passionate improver who experimented with the latest methods of agriculture and horticulture. He introduced new varieties of potato to Culzean and transformed the gardens with planting and architectural features including the ornamental batteries, an idea that had sprung from his father's joke that Culzean could be captured by 'gamekeepers armed with dog whips'. He was a patron of the arts with a good head for business and, although he spent prodigiously, he left almost £200,000 in his will (over £9 million in today's money). Despite all his achievements, however, he died in 1846 a disappointed man. Although he belonged to the Establishment by birth and position, his forceful personality made him an outsider to the men of influence he aspired to join.

THE LIBRARY

THIS ROOM STANDS EXACTLY ON the space occupied by the ground floor of the former tower house, except for a small wing containing a staircase. It used to be known as the Old Eating Room and was part of Earl Thomas's first stage of improvements at Culzean in 1750 when he had created a dining room here, looking out onto the seventeenth-century gardens. In 1877 it became the Library, when the 3rd Marquess decided to swop the functions of this room with the adjacent Adam Library in order to create a new Dining Room next door with better service access from the new kitchens in the west wing.

One of the ceiling roundels, reputedly by Antonio Zucchi.

In the 1770s the room had been redecorated by Robert Adam who introduced classical motifs of fruit and vines to emphasise its function. He also made the proportions of the room more classical by creating the apsidal ends. Originally it conformed to his strict ideas of how eating rooms should be decorated: 'Instead of being hung with damask, tapestry etc. they are always finished with stucco and adorned with statues and paintings that they may not retain the smell of the victuals'. The ceiling was designed in 1779. Although the name of the artist who painted the three ceiling roundels is uncertain, they are of high quality.

When the function of this room and the room next door were swopped in 1877 this room remained largely unaltered. Adam designed the girandoles and the pier glasses between the windows, although there is evidence that the old mirror glass, perhaps dating back to Sir Thomas' time, was re-used. This was common practice as mirror glass was expensive. The fine girandoles for candles in the apses at each end of the room are also by Adam. The six armchairs in simulated bamboo, from Young, Trotter and Hamilton in Edinburgh, placed in this room by the 3rd Marquess, may be the only pieces of documented eighteenth-century furniture at Culzean. It is believed they were acquired by the 11th Earl in 1793. The low, dwarf bookcases were introduced in 1877 when this room became a library and family sitting room.

The firescreen, embroidered with the Kennedy crest, is an interesting feature that was part of an arrangement of screens positioned to prevent heat from the fire melting ladies' wax-based make-up. Wearing make-up in the eighteenth century was a dangerous business. The early deaths of many society beauties were attributed to their pursuit of fashionably white skin which could only be achieved by the application of mercury water or white lead, poisonous substances that could enter the bloodstream.

The Ladies Waldegrave by Sir Joshua Reynolds, 1780, showing the fashionable 'white skin' of the day.

Archibald, 2nd Marquess, in the uniform of colonel of the Ayrshire Yeomanry by Charles Lutyens, 1864. THIS PORTRAIT HANGS IN THE DINING ROOM.

ARCHIBALD KENNEDY
13TH EARL OF CASSILLIS
2ND MARQUESS OF AILSA

The Sportsman Earl

Julia, daughter of Sir Richard Jephson and
wife of the 2nd Marquess of Ailsa.

IN 1846, ANOTHER ARCHIBALD KENNEDY became the 2nd Marquess of Ailsa.
He had already demonstrated his father's propensity for gambling and permission had
been granted by the Court of Session to sell a portion of the Culzean estate to meet his
debts. Without the resources to live on a grand scale, the 2nd Marquess seems then to
have settled down to indulging his chief interests in life – sailing and hunting. He married
Julia Jephson and they had five children.

In 1851 serious financial problems forced the 2nd Marquess to give up living in the south of
England and move to Culzean permanently. Here he lived the life of a typical country
gentleman, shooting, fishing, riding, walking and attending to the estate. In winter, when the
ponds froze, there was curling and hunting. In the summer he sailed. For the first time in many
years Culzean became a family home where the Marquess's children grew up. Other members

The Eglinton Hunt in the late 1860s. The 2nd Marquess of Ailsa can be seen leaning forward, on the right of the two ladies at the right hand side of the pack of hounds.

of the family came often but casual visitors were rare. Indeed Lady Constance, his youngest daughter, recalled that 'they so seldom saw visitors at Culzean that if they happened to hear a carriage come down the driveway, they would all run and hide'.

The 2nd Marquess and his wife divided their time between Culzean and long visits to London, which were made much easier with the arrival of the railway in 1855. The opening of a line from Maybole to Ayr was to bring direct economic benefits to the estate by providing tenants with a route for their produce to Glasgow and its surrounding towns.

When the vineries and conservatories in the walled garden were replaced, the Marquess became very interested in the gardens. He was also of a mechanical bent and installed a workshop in the Castle, the first step towards setting up a boatbuilding business, a project that was brought to fruition by his son.

The four oldest children of the 2nd Marquess by Kenneth Macleay, 1855. From left to right, Alexander (b.1853), Julia (b.1849), Archibald (b.1847, later 3rd Marquess of Ailsa) and Evelyn (b.1851).

According to family tradition, this painting by Charles Towne portrays the 13th Earl of Cassillis.
THIS PAINTING HANGS IN THE BLUE DRAWING ROOM.

The *Kittiwake* at anchor in Aberdeen, a 150 ton schooner, which the Marquess used to sail round the British Isles.

All the honours that his ambitious grandfather had fought so hard for came effortlessly to the 2nd Marquess. In 1859 he was made Knight of the Thistle, the Scottish equivalent of membership of the Garter, an honour that was restricted to the sovereign and sixteen knights. In this capacity he was required to be present at St Giles in Edinburgh on the day of the funeral of Prince Albert. He was also invited to become Colonel of the Ayrshire Yeomanry and, later, Lord Lieutenant of Ayrshire. His duties were mainly to represent the Queen at events in the county and he enjoyed being involved in local affairs.

In March 1870 the Marquess was thrown from his horse whilst out hunting near Kilmarnock. A few days later, he died at Culzean. He is buried in the family graveyard there overlooking the sea.

A Curling Match on Duddingston Loch by Charles Doyle.

CURLING

There were three curling ponds at Culzean and the wider estate and the main one near Sunnyside was still in use until the 1940s. It was rectangular in shape, with shallow water that iced-over quickly. Since the pond was abandoned and drained it has become overgrown, although its shape is still discernible.

Curling is an ancient Scottish sport played between two teams of four. Each player throws two 'stones' with the aim of getting them closest to the centre of a circle, known as a 'house'. The 'house' is 42 yards from the player and as the 'stone' travels this distance, players are allowed to sweep the ice in front of the 'stone' to speed it up so it travels further. 'Stones' can weigh up to 44lbs and the best were made from granite quarried on Ailsa Craig.

THE DINING ROOM

THIS DINING ROOM WAS CREATED BY the 3rd Marquess, who made extensive alterations to the Castle in 1877. It has great importance in the history of taste and possibly marks the first time in Britain that new work in a genuine Adam house was carried out in a harmonising Adam Revival style.

In the original Adam design this room was two rooms with a partition to the left of the fireplace. The larger space was the Library, the smaller a dressing room or business room. Only the frieze, the stucco medallions and tablets on the south wall remain from the Adam period. In the 1870s the cornice was copied and ingeniously extended around the newly enlarged room whilst the chimneypiece and the door cases are replicas of those in the Eating Room.

Archibald Kennedy, Earl of Cassillis (1794-1832), by John Ferneley Senior. Eldest son of the 1st Marquess of Ailsa, whom he predeceased by fourteen years. The 1st Marquess's title passed directly to his grandson, Archibald.
THIS PORTRAIT HANGS IN THE DINING ROOM.

The Kennedys, like many other aristocrats at the time, were members of the Fancy, a fast set much given to gambling. The father of the 2nd Marquess, Archibald, Lord Kennedy, was fond of making elaborate wagers usually connected to sporting feats. Not surprisingly he managed to accumulate over £150,000 of gambling debts in ten years (the equivalent of several million pounds today). Perhaps fortunately for the future of Culzean, he died in 1832, a month after his wife had given birth to their tenth child. She died shortly after, leaving the 1st Marquess to bring up their children.

The ceiling is a copy in papier maché of a ceiling designed by Adam for the music room of a house in St James Square, London. It was based on an illustration published in Adam's *Works in Architecture*. It was made by Jackson & Sons in London who specialised in papier maché ceilings and emerged as Robert Adam Revival experts.

The pictures, mainly of Kennedy forebears, are largely hung as they were by the 3rd Marquess with the arrangement over the fireplace replicating a photograph from *Country Life* of 1915. The 3rd Marquess continued to refine the Adam character of this room all his life, for example placing pairs of neoclassical vases and female plaster figures on each doorcase, a reminder of an arrangement once found in Adam's original Library bookcases.

The Troubadour firescreen in Berlin Woolwork was made by Julia, Marchioness of Ailsa, the mother of the 3rd Marquess who must have commissioned its elegant Adam Revival frame to help it blend in with his otherwise stylistically faithful room.

The Dining Room photographed for *Country Life* in 1915.

The 3rd Marquess by Anthony Carey
Stannus, 1875 *(detail)*.
THIS PORTRAIT HANGS IN THE EISENHOWER APARTMENT.

ARCHIBALD KENNEDY

14TH EARL OF CASSILLIS
3RD MARQUESS OF AILSA

The Sailor Earl

The *Foxhound* racing against the *Vanguard* in 1870 near Land's End by A.W. Fowles, 1870. THIS PAINTING HANGS IN THE GENTLEMAN'S STATE DRESSING ROOM.

ARCHIBALD KENNEDY SUCCEEDED TO THE TITLE and the Culzean estate at the age of 22 and for the rest of his long life devoted himself to his twin passions – sailing and the improvement of his beloved Culzean.

Evelyn Stuart, who became the first wife of the 3rd Marquess of Ailsa, 1866.

No one growing up at Culzean could fail to be awed by the majesty of the sea and mountains of the Ayrshire coast. The 3rd Marquess, the first to actually spend his childhood at the Castle, was no exception. From boyhood he had been a keen sailor and his sailing career covered what has been described as the Golden Age of yachting – the years between 1870 and the turn of the century when yachting was transformed from an amateur pastime into the chosen sport of kings and the wealthy. During this time too, yacht design and building became a science around which there was much experimentation fuelled by intense rivalry to build boats that could win races. The 3rd Marquess was at the heart of all this, both as a championship-winning sailor and as a notable designer and innovator.

The 3rd Marquess owned several fine racing yachts including the *Foxhound*, *Bloodhound* and *Sleuthound*, all built at Fife's yard up the coast at Fairlie. He was a member of at least nine yacht clubs and was qualified as a Master Mariner. He also commanded the Clyde Royal Navy Volunteer Reserves in his own steam yachts, the *Marquesa* and the *Titania*.

In 1871 the 3rd Marquess married Evelyn, daughter of Lord Blantyre. She was a devout Christian and part of an upper-class evangelical set committed to good works and teetotalism. The Ailsas embarked on major building works at Culzean partly in order to accommodate their expanding family.

Evelyn died in 1888 and the Marquess, broken-hearted, shut up Culzean and spent most of the next few years abroad in Africa, India and Sweden, as well as some time in London. In 1891 he met and married Isabella MacMaster, by whom he had two more children.

The *Sleuthound* winning the Queen's Cup at Cowes, by Barlow Moore, 1882. (*detail*)
THIS WATERCOLOUR HANGS IN THE GENTLEMAN'S STATE DRESSING ROOM.

The *Beagle* in the boatyard on the shore at Culzean, 1880.

The 3rd Marquess was charged with breaking the speed limit of 20 miles per hour by driving at 31 miles per hour on a stretch of road between Temple Sowerby and Penrith. He defended himself against the charge by claiming that, as he had to increase his speed to get uphill at the time, he might well have exceeded the speed limit slightly but not as much as the police claimed. He was fined £2 and costs.

By this time a long agricultural depression had set in. The 3rd Marquess spent a great deal of energy trying to find alternative sources of income for the estate and get it out of its never-ending financial difficulties. His approach was erratic. He would think nothing of commissioning an expensive yacht that he could ill afford. At the same time he often came up with remarkably hard-headed commercial ventures. In 1871 a new boathouse was constructed at Culzean to accommodate a boatbuilding and repairing business which later evolved into the Ailsa Shipbuilding Company in nearby Troon. Until its closure in 2000, the company was one of Scotland's most successful boatyards, with commissions that ranged from the famous Mersey ferry boats to luxury yachts for the King of Belgium and the wealthy Vanderbilt family. Another success was his development of Turnberry Golf Course and Hotel. Becoming a golf fanatic late in life, Lord Ailsa had initially laid out private links at Culzean. He later established a championship course at Turnberry and then convinced his fellow directors on the Glasgow and South Western Railway to build a new line that would go to Turnberry and a new hotel especially for golfers, a radically innovative idea at the time. The railway line and hotel opened in 1901 and Turnberry is still one the UK's most luxurious resort hotels.

Despite all Lord Ailsa's best efforts, however, the estate continued to lurch from crisis to crisis. In 1933, faced with increased taxation and the possibility of enormous death duties, the decision was taken to disentail the estate and create a limited company with family members as its directors. This would save large sums in tax and was approved by the heir to Culzean, the 15th Earl, and his brothers who would later inherit the estate. In 1938 Lord Ailsa, aged 90 and confined to a wheelchair, died at Culzean. It was the end of an era.

The Nursery Wing at Culzean, added by Wardrop & Reid in 1877.

THE BUILDING OF THE WEST WING

In 1877 the 3rd Marquess embarked on a large-scale programme of modernisation at Culzean. Very little had been done to the house for over sixty years and the Marchioness, used to luxurious homes, considered it expensive to heat and not very comfortable. She also wanted new nursery accommodation for her expanding family.

The 3rd Marquess commissioned Edinburgh architects Wardrop & Reid to produce designs for a new wing. Their work at Haddo House in Aberdeenshire was considered first-rate and in keeping with the spirit of Adam. At Culzean, Adam's Brewhouse Wing was converted into a new Nursery Wing connected on three floors to the existing house. It had new rooms for the children, a new kitchen and new servants' quarters. The main Castle entrance was enlarged with a new portico, offices and plan rooms. The Library and Dressing Room became a new Dining Room whilst the Old Eating Room was turned into a Library. Wherever possible, original Adam fittings were reused or new ones made in the Adam style.

In addition to the structural work the principal rooms were redecorated. Pictures and mirrors were regilded and much of the furniture reupholstered. The total cost of the whole project was over £20,000 – the equivalent of almost £1 million today. The outcome of all this work was to be a house that, for a long time, was one of the grandest houses in Ayrshire.

'O gallant was our "forty"
from her brazen rudder head
To her fighting flag a chevron
and her keel of solid lead
She looked every inch a lady
when we sailed her for the line
And no "forty" on the water
the Bloodhound could outshine.'

Verse from a poem to his boat, the *Bloodhound,* written by the 3rd Marquess of Ailsa.

The *Bloodhound* gybing in the Royal Irish Regatta off Kingston, 1909.

The *Bloodhound,* nicknamed the *Dog,* was a racing machine and the 3rd Marquess of Ailsa won over £2,000 in prize money in her. To celebrate the *Bloodhound's* best season in 1877 he commissioned the solid silver clock that can be seen in the Dining Room of the Castle.

THE OVAL STAIRCASE

THE OVAL STAIRCASE AT CULZEAN DISPLAYS Robert Adam at his innovative best. So logical is his design for this oval, colonnaded staircase with light pouring in from above that it would seem that the entire house was built to accommodate it. In truth, building the Oval Staircase was the final stage of the Adam design of Culzean, giving dynamic unity to a house whose disparate parts reflected the difficulties of developing an ancient fortified site.

Napoleon by Robert Lefèvre. This portrait was acquired by the 1st Marquess on his travels in Europe after the Napoleonic War. As soon as the war ended, the British upper classes flocked to France and Belgium to visit the battlefields and sites connected with Napoleon and to acquire paintings and objects related to him.

THIS PORTRAIT HANGS IN THE OVAL STAIRCASE.

RIGHT The Temple of Jupiter at Emperor Diocletian's ruined palace in Spalatro, which inspired Adam's Oval Staircase.

BELOW Adam's plans for the Oval Staircase.

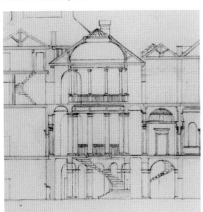

The staircase also allowed access to all the Castle's new public rooms from one central point and replaced the front and back staircases that lay between the original house and the new north-facing drum tower. And it was oval largely because there was no room for the more traditional circular staircase.

Adam's choice of the imperial stairway leading from the ground to the main floor completed his vision of the Oval Staircase as a magnificent theatrical setting. It is almost certain that the 1st Marquess, who completed the Oval Staircase after Adam's death, took the decision to reverse the traditional architectural order of the twelve pillars on each floor of the staircase to place the Corinthian columns below the Ionic whilst the Doric remain on the ground floor. This had the advantage of positioning the richer, more decorative style on the main floor of the house to be admired by all. At the same time the pillars create a simple trick of perspective to make the space seem much bigger than it actually is.

On the main floor of the staircase are large-scale portraits of the 1st Marquess and Marchioness and a portrait of Napoleon by Robert Lefèvre, acquired by the 1st Marquess on his travels in Europe after the Napoleonic War. The 1st Marquess left specific instructions in his will for the painting of Napoleon to be taken to Culzean. All three portraits are now hung as they were in the nineteenth century and are protected by brass rails that were probably made in the 3rd Marquess's boatyards.

THE ROUND DRAWING ROOM

ROBERT ADAM'S DESIGN FOR THIS unique room perfectly reflects his notions that buildings should complement their surroundings. Inside are all the characteristics of eighteenth-century elegance: outside lies the wild, dramatic scenery of the Ayrshire coast.

The Round Drawing Room, formerly referred to by Adam as the Saloon, was completed only after Adam's death and details of the ceiling and plasterwork conform more to 1820s Regency aesthetic standards than to the work done under Adam's supervision. It is clear that there can have been few surviving working drawings for this room. The 3rd Marquess later carried out his own Adam style redecoration, most notably combining eighteenth-century girandoles with

later Adam Revival ones. Of the marble busts in Adam's niches, the one to the left of the door to the Oval Staircase is Pauline Borghese Buonaparte, the one on the right is Caroline Murat Buonaparte. The bust on the table is Elisa Baciocchi Buonaparte. All three women were Napoleon's sisters. The paintings in this room celebrate Kennedy women.

This room has been arranged in a formal way with giltwood chairs positioned around the sides to better display the grandeur of the space. It was designed to come into its own on grand social occasions. In the daytime visitors would have congregated to admire the spectacular panoramic views whilst French windows opening onto the balcony transformed the room into a belvedere during warmer weather. One can easily imagine how Earl David would have envisaged glittering evening occasions. Guests in their finery would climb the magnificent Oval Staircase to be received formally by their host on the piano nobile, the principal floor of the house. Then they would circulate through the procession of state apartments, admiring decorative details as they went from room to room. The Round Drawing Room would have been a focal point.

Bagniggi Wells, Finsbury, London, on a Sunday Evening by John Sanders, 1779.

In the 1770s, when Culzean was built, fashions had reached the height of ornamentation. For men this meant embroidered waistcoats and jackets in velvet and satin, lace cravats, knee breeches, clocked stockings and high shoes with jewelled buckles. Women's clothes were even more elaborate, with layers of petticoats and ruffled skirts in silk and velvet topped with silk bodices and open robes, decorated with braid and jewels. Both sexes favoured pomaded and powdered hairstyles, with women's styles sometimes rising three feet into the air. They were either wigs or natural hair built over horsehair pads and wire cages and decorated with feathers, ribbons, jewels, and even stuffed birds.

Susanna, Countess of Eglinton attributed to Gavin Hamilton. Commissioned by the 9th Earl. Susanna was the daughter of Sir Archibald 'the wicked' of Culzean and aunt of the 9th Earl. She was the third wife of the Earl of Eglinton and survived her husband by 57 years, living to the remarkable age of 90. Susanna Eglinton was a noted beauty of her day. The famous Dr Johnson met her, aged 84, and described her as 'a very agreeable woman. She was of the noble house of Kennedy and had all the elevation which the consciousness of such birth inspires.' *Life of Samuel Johnson* by James Boswell.

THIS PORTRAIT HANGS IN THE ROUND DRAWING ROOM.

THE STATE BEDROOM AND DRESSING ROOMS

THIS SUITE OF ROOMS IS ENTERED from the anteroom. Although there are no surviving Adam drawings for this part of Culzean, some of their finishing may have been done under his supervision. A bill approved by Adam in 1791 includes a description of what appears to be the chimneypiece of the Round Drawing Room anteroom with '1 Urn and 2 Sphinx'. At that time it was described as the 'Octagon Anti Room'. By the time of the 1st Marquess, this room had become the Gentleman's State Dressing Room, the first of a suite of state apartments.

This gentleman's wardrobe splits in two, for ease of movement.

Robert Adam approved the design of this fireplace in 1791 and the bright steel grate was supplied by Larnder of London.

Another bill for chimneypieces approved by Adam in 1791 identifies the next room as 'L. C. Bedroom'. If the 10th Earl had been used to one of the bedrooms in his brother's clifftop office wing with its dramatic sea views, it is easy to see why he might have chosen this room for his own use. It is equally easy to see how it was chosen by the 1st Marquess as his State Bedchamber for use by Culzean's most important guests.

In this Bedroom the cheval mirror, one of two at Culzean, remain from the 1st Marquess's comprehensive Regency furnishing of the state rooms at Culzean. The 3rd Marquess was keen to stamp an earlier Georgian character on this room and may have introduced the Chippendale four-post bed and the handsome gentleman's wardrobe, dating from the 1740s.

The Lady's State Dressing Room is a plain and awkwardly shaped room built around one of Adam's existing round corner towers where the chimneypiece is now. The corner press opposite the fireplace was adapted to provide a late Victorian water closet.

The Fire Pond

When it was built, Culzean was equipped with every modern convenience possible. Adam's original plans detail the plumbing for lavatories and cold water taps that were installed right up to the top floor, with drains leading out over the cliff. The water to supply them was piped in from the reservoir (now the Fire Pond) located on a hill above the castle. Around this time Joseph Bramah had perfected a design for a flushing lavatory, similar to modern versions, which might well have been chosen for Culzean. In the brewhouse block (where the west wing is now) there was a bathhouse with deep marble hot and cold baths.

THE BLUE DRAWING ROOM

THE FIRST OF THE SERIES OF GRAND STATEROOMS designed by Robert Adam, this room looks now very much as it would have done at the end of the eighteenth century, with the colour scheme representing what was then fashionable.

Adam designed the chimneypiece in pure white statuary marble in 1778. Its delicate execution and diminutively scaled ornaments contrast with the bolder forms of the later Round Drawing Room chimneypiece. Unusually for an Adam design, the ceiling incorporates four sculptural bas-relief panels shaped to reflect the curves of the ellipse. The central painted panel may depict Venus chastising Cupid.

In the Blue Drawing Room is the Plenary Indulgence *(detail shown)*, a papal pardon obtained from Pope Benedict XIV by Sir Thomas Kennedy in the early 1750s during his stay in Rome.

By the late eighteenth century the arrangement of a Georgian country house had increasingly begun to reflect women's interests. The dining room had become a male zone, a place where men lingered after dinner to enjoy their brandy and cigars. Ladies retreated to a 'withdrawing room' to drink tea, coffee and chocolate until they were joined by the men. In a generic description Robert Adam describes his design for a drawing room as: 'an admirable room for the reception of the company before dinner, or for the ladies to retire to after it ...' (*Works in Architecture*, Volume 1).

The room's furnishings represent almost every period of Culzean's history. Over the fireplace hangs William Mosman's fine portrait of Sir Thomas Kennedy, one of Culzean's most celebrated paintings. *The Lion and the Mouse* by Frans Snyders hangs on the north wall. The long, low bookcase is made up from two Regency chiffoniers, survivors of the Regency furnishings of the Castle. The suite of Grecian giltwood furniture was presented to the National Trust for Scotland by Lady MacTaggart Stewart, the sister-in-law of the 4th Marquess.

The Lion and the Mouse by the studio of Paul de Vos. THIS PAINTING HANGS IN THE BLUE DRAWING ROOM.

The brass mounted rosewood writing table may conceivably have been at Culzean since the early nineteenth century. It is attributed to the London cabinet-maker, John Maclean.

On the north wall hangs one of Culzean's most celebrated paintings, a magnificent pictorial representation of Aesop's fable of *The Lion and the Mouse*. Believed in the nineteenth and early twentieth centuries to be the work of Rubens, the painting is today attributed to the Flemish master Frans Snyders, one of the finest animal painters of his day and a close friend of Rubens, with whom he collaborated on numerous projects. A different version of this canvas ascribed to the hands of both Rubens and Snyders is in the collection of Chequers, the country seat of the British Prime Minister. During the 1st Marquess of Ailsa's lifetime, the Culzean painting hung in London, but in line with specific instructions laid down by the 1st Marquess in his will, was dispatched to Scotland following the death of his wife, Margaret, in 1847. We know from photographic and written evidence that the painting was displayed on this wall of the castle during the 3rd Marquess's lifetime.

THE LONG DRAWING ROOM

THIS ROOM WAS THE GREAT HALL of the medieval castle. In his 1777 plans, Adam refers to it as the 'Picture Room', perhaps intending to display art treasures acquired by Sir Thomas Kennedy on his grand tour. By the late 1780s the building of the Oval Staircase required the fireplace to be moved and the central doorway broken through in its place. For obvious reasons it had become known, by 1846, as the Long Drawing Room.

ALEXANDER NASMYTH
(1758-1840)

Born in Edinburgh in 1758, Alexander Nasmyth became one of the most influential and sought after Scottish landscape painters of his time. At the age of 16 he was discovered by Allan Ramsay, under whom he trained as a portraitist in London. Following travels in Italy, Nasmyth set himself up as a portrait painter in Edinburgh, and was soon in demand amongst aristocrats and merchants of the city. He was a friend and collaborator of Robert Burns, whom he painted on at least two occasions.

However, Nasmyth is best known for his monumental classical landscapes and this view of Culzean is typical of his mature style.

Culzean from the east by Alexander Nasmyth. THIS PAINTING HANGS IN THE LONG DRAWING ROOM.

The room now displays some of the finest marine pictures associated with Culzean, an appropriate theme for a house so closely connected in every way with the sea. Of particular note are the two marvellous views of Culzean, in sumptuous Regency frames, by Alexander Nasmyth, one of Scotland's most famous painters. They were commissioned by the 1st Marquess as part of a series of large panoramas of Culzean, many of which were intended as presents for his family or to be hung at his London homes. In these paintings the height of the cliffs has been greatly exaggerated to make the castle appear even more wild and romantic than it actually is. We can be sure that the 1st Marquess would have prominently displayed them to emphasise to all the grandeur of his family's Scottish estates.

Other nautical subjects in this room are the portraits of the 11th Earl and the 3rd Marquess in naval uniform and *A View of the Frigate HMS* London *in a Breeze off Shakespeare Cliff, Dover* by Thomas Luny. The other small seascapes include one painted in 1845 by Nicholas Matthew Condy showing Queen Victoria and Prince Albert and their four children in a barge off Osborne House. There are also a number of paintings and watercolours of the 3rd Marquess's ships.

The oriental carpet is the only original carpet at Culzean to remain in situ and must have been woven especially for the room.

This model of the French frigate *Hortense,* now in the Library, is said to have been made by French prisoners-of-war confined in Porchester Castle from the 'bones of their beef rations', *circa* 1800.

LADY AILSA'S BOUDOIR
AND THE DRESSING ROOM

IN THE 1777 REBUILDING OF CULZEAN this room was intended to be the principal or 'Best Bedroom' coming at the end of the suite of formal reception rooms with its dressing room next door. Adam's frieze here appropriately depicts poppy seed heads, emblematic of sleep. After the new north front to the Castle was completed, new State Apartments were built on the other side of the house (see State Bedroom on p46). The 3rd Marquess and Marchioness used these rooms as family rooms with the bedroom becoming Lady Ailsa's Boudoir. In 2011, the National Trust for Scotland refurbished these rooms, along with the Wardrobe Room and the Family Bedroom.

Lord John Kennedy by Charles Lutyens, 1864. He was the youngest son of the 2nd Marquess, and is painted here, aged five standing by the Swan Pond at Culzean. Charles Lutyens also painted the fine equestrian portrait of the 2nd Marquess, now in the Dining Room. Lutyens and the 2nd Marquess shared a passion for hunting and riding and struck up a firm friendship during the artist 's extended stay at Culzean from 1863-4.

THIS PORTRAIT HANGS IN LADY ALISA'S BOUDOIR.

A bell pull was located in every room used by the family in the Castle. They were linked by a pulley system to bells on the wall outside the kitchen in the servants' quarters where they can still be seen. Each bell was numbered so that the servants would know which room to go to.

In the 1870s these rooms were extended into a private family suite, with the Marchioness's rooms leading into a 'Family Bedroom' overlooking the sea, adjoined by the Marquess's Dressing Room, Wardrobe Room and Bathroom and leading on into the children's rooms in the new West Wing.

At that time too, the chimneypiece from the Library, designed by Adam in 1778, was relocated here. It is exceptionally fine, with its figurative tablets depicting Minerva and classical motifs of learning. Adam's original Library mirror now hangs over it.

In keeping with the intimate family character of the rooms a selection of personal portraits of female family members and children are displayed here. In 2011 the Trust uncovered the original Adam chimneypiece in the Family Bedroom.

Lady Ailsa's Dressing Room now houses some important pieces of Adam decoration such as the chimneypiece and accompanying chimney glass, which was designed in 1782 by Adam. The oval pier mirror, also designed by Adam, hangs above a very rare concave pine dressing table that was probably used when powdering hair.

This room is now the 'Adam Room' of the Castle and is home to changing displays of architectural drawings relating to the Castle and the estate. The breakfront bookcase contains architectural fragments from the successive decorative schemes at the Castle.

THE KITCHEN

THE KITCHEN AT CULZEAN IS THE ORIGINAL KITCHEN block designed by Adam in 1777 and was used for almost 100 years, until the West Wing of the castle was built in the 1870s. Fear of fire required the kitchen to be separated from the house and Adam integrated his design to the north-east side of the existing buildings, creating a two-storey building ending in a large semi-circular bow that looks more like a chapel than a kitchen.

When the 1st Marquess and his family were in residence, kitchen staff worked long hours, rising early to light the fires and sometimes staying up late to provide a light supper around 11 pm. Two main meals were prepared – breakfast and dinner. Breakfast was served between 9 and 10 am

ICE HOUSES

Culzean had at least two ice houses, built around 1780. One was under the Viaduct and the other was to the east of the Swan Pond. During winter, when the Swan Pond had iced over, two men in a flat-bottomed boat would break the ice into blocks using pick-axes and guide the ice into an inlet by the ice house. Estate workers would then collect the ice in wire baskets and load it onto carts which took it to the ice stores. Collecting ice in this way continued at Culzean until just before World War I.

The ice was packed in straw which acted as insulation, and then left until the warmer months when it was taken to the Castle for cooling drinks, preserving food and making ice-cream. The ice house in the Viaduct was used as an outside larder and was still in use in the early 1900s.

either in the small Buffet Room or, if there were guests, in the Eating Room. It usually consisted of cold meats and various breads served with tea, coffee and hot chocolate.

Breakfast was simple compared to dinner, especially a formal one (see below for a description of a Regency dinner). Then the cooking went on all day. Menus were planned well in advance and many ingredients were local. The gardens and Home Farm of Culzean produced an enormous variety of fruit, vegetables, meat, eggs and poultry and there would have been no shortage of fish, game and oysters from the oyster beds on the shore.

Between noon and 2 pm everything was cleaned and prepared. Meats would be put to roast on spits by the fire. The oven by the side of the range was used for baking while the stewing stoves under the far windows were used to prepare sauces, stocks and soups. Once all the food was ready, the kitchen table would be laid out with the dishes exactly as they were meant to stand on the dining-room table.

In addition to providing meals for the family and guests this kitchen would have to cater for the staff. There was a strict hierarchy amongst the servants and those at the top of the social pecking order got the best food. Most important of all was the cook. Good cooks were the best paid servants in the house and worth their weight in gold. It's not difficult to see why.

The Dinner Party by Sir Henry Cole.

By the 1820s dinner was the main meal of the day and was served between 5 and 7pm. Usually the first course would be various different types of meat like stewed venison, roast beef, turkey, game and veal. Sometimes soup or fish dishes would accompany them and, if so, would be eaten first. Vegetables featured only as a garnish. The second course would be lighter dishes of meat and fish with sweet pies, puddings and tarts. All the dishes were placed in a pre-arranged order on the table. Liveried footmen served guests by taking their plates to the dishes. 'Remove' dishes of biscuits and pickles would be placed on the table between courses. The tablecloth was taken away before the dessert course of jellies, sweetmeats, nuts and cheese, ice-cream and sorbets.

Archibald Kennedy, 4th Marquess of Ailsa by William Edwards Miller.

The 4th Marquess had trained as a barrister but his wife's wealth and a modest allowance from his father meant he was free to pursue his own interests. He was a dedicated Freemason, a keen shot and an enthusiastic fisherman. He developed an interest in Scottish history and was a fluent Gaelic speaker.
THIS PAINTING HANGS IN THE DINING ROOM.

THE LAST OWNERS OF CULZEAN

The End of an Era

ARCHIBALD KENNEDY, WHO BECAME the 4th Marquess of Ailsa in 1938, had spent little time at Culzean. When his mother died, he and the other children had been sent off to Castle Grant in Aberdeenshire, the home of their great aunt, the Countess of Seafield. Here they were brought up with almost no contact with their father until his remarriage, when the 3rd Marquess and his new bride returned to live at Culzean.

Before he succeeded to the title the 4th Marquess lived for many years at Newhailes, near Musselburgh, East Lothian, another property now in the care of the National Trust for Scotland.

As the heir, the 4th Marquess had agreed to dissolve the entail on the Culzean and Cassillis estates and turn them into a family business but he knew that it was not a long-term solution. By the time he himself inherited, he was worried about the future of Culzean. He had no children and was convinced that neither he nor his heir, his brother Charles, could afford to run the estate. Although he had no intention of living at Culzean permanently, he was proud of the connection between Culzean and the Kennedys and wanted to preserve its history. Accordingly he approached the newly formed National Trust for Scotland to discuss handing over the Castle to the nation. In 1943, before any decision was taken, the 4th Marquess died.

Ironically our story of Culzean Castle, the Culzean Kennedys and the Earls of Cassillis began with three brothers inheriting in turn and ended the same way. Archibald, the 4th Marquess was succeeded by his brother Charles, who was followed by his brother Angus, the 6th Marquess (above) in 1956. He never lived at Culzean.

General Eisenhower visiting Culzean in 1946 with the 5th Marquess, who is on the far left.

When he inherited, the 5th Marquess was very comfortably settled in his wife's country house and estate in Dumfriesshire and had as little inclination to live at Culzean as his brother. He too was childless. In 1945 a meeting took place between the representatives of the Kennedy family and the National Trust for Scotland. Lady Frances, the widow of the 4th Marquess, did most of the negotiating and agreement was reached to hand over the castle, the policies, the gardens and the Home Farm to the Trust. The Marquess was keen that the top floor of the castle should be converted into a flat for the use of General Eisenhower as a gesture of Scottish thanks for America's support during World War II. It was also stipulated that Lady Frances should have lifetime use of the west wing. These conditions were willingly met and Culzean was formally handed over to the National Trust for Scotland in 1945.

THE ESTATE AND HOME FARM

GREAT DYNASTIES LIKE THE KENNEDY FAMILY were sustained by their relationship with the land. Ownership of land defined them and gave them wealth and political power.

The foundation of many large estates dated back to the granting of land to noblemen as a reward for their loyalty (as with Sir Thomas Kennedy). They derived their income from renting out the land to tenant farmers, keeping one farm to provide food for the household.

In the eighteenth century the agricultural revolution introduced new ideas to farming and the landed classes developed a passion for what were called 'improvements'. At Culzean, under the influence of Earl Thomas and Earl David, stone walls were constructed and hedges planted to enclose the land and create large fields in order to eradicate the old system of strip cultivation. Farms were amalgamated into larger units and trees were planted as wind breaks and game coverts. Land was converted into pasture for the rearing of the cattle for which Ayrshire was becoming famous. Drainage was introduced and tenants' leases specified that they must use new agricultural techniques like crop rotation and soil improvement. Professional factors ran the estates, collected rents and advised on what investment should be made. The fishing and shooting was let to bring in extra income. These new methods boosted food output and allowed the estate to increase rents dramatically. In 1754 the rental income from the farms on the Culzean estate was £640 plus produce (the equivalent of around £64,000 per annum today). By 1775 it had risen almost four-fold to £2,270 a year.

The Home Farm at Culzean was run on model lines and supplied food for the whole house with the surplus sold locally. Around 1778, when the Castle was being rebuilt, new farm buildings were constructed to Adam's design. They were a showpiece with the most modern facilities, estate offices and homes for the farm workers.

Home Farm during restoration in 1971.

The fully restored Home Farm houses the Visitor Centre, shop, restaurant and Park offices.

The Orangery.
Culzean was always almost totally self-sufficient in food production. Supplies from the estate were sent to the family, wherever they were, and the household records detail regular shipments to London of game, meat, butter, eggs, and fruit including exotics like pineapples, vegetables and flowers.

Alfred Harrison, Head Gardener at Culzean from 1919 (in trilby) and garden staff.

Until the agricultural depression of the 1880s, rents from the estate provided a substantial income, although there were often financial difficulties. The increasing unprofitability of agriculture combined with escalating taxation, introduced by the Liberal Government in 1909, led to the grim realisation that owning and living in a house like Culzean was no longer possible for one family without other sources of income. Fortunately Culzean Castle and its unique surroundings have been preserved for the nation. Many other country houses and estates throughout Scotland were not.

GAS HOUSE

As part of an earlier drive to reduce costs, a gasworks had been built on the shore of Culzean by the 2nd Marquess. Coal was brought by boat to the Gas House where the gas was extracted in the furnace and then piped to the Castle and Home Farm. In the 1870s, this system was modernised to provide all the heating and lighting for the castle.

In the early 1900s the fuel was converted to cleaner acetylene gas which was used at Culzean until the 1950s when the Castle was finally connected to electricity. The Gas House fell into disrepair but was restored in 1993 and now houses exhibitions on gas production and the life of William Murdoch, the inventor of gas lighting who, coincidentally, was born nearby.

THE GARDENS AND POLICIES OF CULZEAN

IN 1969 THE GROUNDS OF CULZEAN CASTLE were declared Scotland's first Country Park. A spectacular example of the 'designed' landscape of a great country estate, it covers over 600 acres of woodland, formal gardens and important architecture as well as three miles of varied coastline. This blend of exciting history and a superb natural setting is a major attraction for Culzean's many visitors.

LEFT The Swan Pond.
CENTRE The Walled Garden.
RIGHT The Dolphin House with the Round House in the foreground.

The Viaduct bridges the glen and is supported by six arches interspersed with towers. Leading into it is the Ruined Arch, a folly deliberately built as a ruin to remind visitors of the Kennedys' ancient lineage.

When the Tower House at Culzean was first built, its immediate surroundings were purely defensive. As Ayrshire became a more peaceful place these were gradually transformed. Sir Archibald Kennedy, Laird of Culzean in the late seventeenth century, laid out gardens (where the Fountain Court is now) which were described as '... very pretty gardens and orchards, adorned with excellent tarases [terraces] and the walls loaden with peaches, apricotes, cherries, and other fruits ...'.

Later, when the Castle was being rebuilt, David Kennedy wanted to create an appropriate setting for his new home. He and Robert Adam were much influenced by the then fashionable notions of the Picturesque, which held that landscape should be full of curious details, interesting contrast, surprise and enchantment.

The Ruined Arch at the entrance of the Viaduct leading to Culzean Castle.

In keeping with these ideas, the immediate approach to the Castle was designed as an experience. Visitors descended the hill and caught sight of the castle in the distance with its towers and battlements framed within the ruined archway. Crossing the Viaduct, they passed under another arch and were confronted with a dramatic vista of the sea and sky before arriving at the castle entrance. Adam's plans for the Viaduct and Ruined Arch were inspired, it is believed, by the ruins of Hadrian's Villa outside Rome and there is evidence that they were built with materials from the demolished sections of the old tower house.

The Walled Garden with its kitchen and pleasure gardens was first laid out between 1775 and 1786. Bricks were used to line the stone walls in order to retain heat. The kitchen garden was ultra-modern for its time with greenhouses built against the central hollow spine wall, which

LEFT Underground heating for the greenhouses.
CENTRE The Walled Garden around 1945.
RIGHT Hollow walls in the greenhouse enabled the movement of hot air to provide an ideal temperature for growth.

The restored Cat Gates.

The Servants' Walkway runs between the Castle and the Clock Tower Courtyard and was built to ensure that the servants and visiting tradesmen could not be seen by the family or guests arriving at the front door.

was heated by flues. A Vinery was constructed to grow grapes indoors. This has been fully restored to its later Victorian splendour.

The well known landscape gardener, Thomas White Senior, a pupil of the famous 'Capability' Brown, took over the design of the garden and policies around 1790. In typical White fashion there was a long and theatrical approach from Maybole via Pennyglen Lodge and Hoolity Ha', and a second, equally attractive, entrance route from Kirkoswald via Morriston Lodge and the Cat Gates. There are no less than 40 small architectural features scattered through the vast grounds of the Culzean estate. Almost all of them were built in the time of the 1st Marquess, a keen horticulturalist who also oversaw the planting of over five million trees and laid out walkways flanked by rare shrubs.

The Round House, a small stone changing hut on the beach, constructed in the early nineteenth century to enjoy the new fashion for sea-bathing.

The Pagoda, *circa* 1880.

The Dolphin House, built as a laundry in the 1840s, is the first example of Adam Revival building at Culzean. It was linked to the Castle by a pathway across the steep cliffside. The laundry area consisted of a low washroom with washtubs along one side of the room and boilers on the other side, and a tall drying room. In fine weather clothes were hung outside to dry. Three laundry maids lived at Dolphin House and coped with all the household washing. The building is now a residential outdoor educational facility run by South Ayrshire Council.

The original Deer Park, established by the 3rd Marquess, was home to a variety of unusual animals such as ostriches, an emu, a herd of buffalo and a collection of Belgian goats. It was a Victorian fashion to breed exotic animals and birds and the 1st Marquess had earlier created an aviary at the Swan Pond.

The Cedar of Lebanon in the South Walled Garden.

Over the years, particularly as game rearing became more profitable, the grounds were filled with plantations and game coverts. The 2nd and 3rd Marquesses continued the tradition of large-scale plantings.

From the earliest days of Culzean, each Kennedy generation made its own highly individual contribution until gradually, over the centuries, the policies evolved into the unique landscape of today. Since the National Trust for Scotland took over their stewardship in 1945, it has been very conscious of maintaining this tradition. Public funding has enabled the grounds to be restored to their former glory. But landscape is a living thing and the work of the Trust in restoring, conserving, planting and opening up forgotten vistas, continues.

The herbaceous border in the Walled Garden in midsummer bloom.

THE NATIONAL TRUST FOR SCOTLAND

THE NATIONAL TRUST FOR SCOTLAND is Scotland's leading conservation organisation. It is not a government department, but a charity supported by its membership of over 310,000. The Trust was founded in 1931 by a small group of Scots concerned at the growing threat to the country's natural and built heritage. Now it is an influential body with more than a hundred diverse properties. Its remit, set out in various Acts of Parliament, is to promote the care and conservation of the Scottish landscape and historic buildings while providing access for the public to enjoy them.

Over 76,000 hectares of beautiful and dramatic countryside are in the Trust's care, as are over 50 buildings of historical, architectural and social importance. The future of this heritage depends on our ability to meet ever-increasing financial demands. We can do this only with the help of our membership. Please support our valuable work by becoming a member, making a donation or arranging a legacy.

Join at any property, online at www.nts.org.uk, or by contacting the Membership Department on 0844 493 2100 or email membership@nts.org.uk

THE EISENHOWER AT CULZEAN

The Eisenhower at Culzean Castle is named after General Dwight D Eisenhower, who was gifted the use of the top floor of the castle as a thank you for his leadership of the Allied Forces during World War II. General Eisenhower took up residence at Culzean for the first time in the autumn of 1946, flying into Prestwick Airport on 1 October. On this visit General Eisenhower was accompanied by Mrs Eisenhower, their son John D Eisenhower and Mrs Eisenhower's mother, Mrs John Sheldon Doud. 'Ike' visited a further three times, once during his second term as President of the USA when Culzean became his Scottish 'White House'.

All six rooms have been tastefully upgraded, whilst retaining the country house style, with many original furnishings from the Kennedy family. Guests can choose to stay in one bedroom and enjoy the country house ambience with other guests who are staying, or take the Eisenhower in its entirety for a family gathering, wedding or anniversary celebration, or birthday party.

The elegant circular Drawing Room boasts breathtaking panoramic views across the Firth of Clyde towards the Isle of Arran – and on a clear day you might even catch a glimpse of the coast of Northern Ireland. All Eisenhower guests share the use of this delightful room, which has ample comfortable seating, allowing intimate conversations or a larger gathering in front of the fireplaces. The Eisenhower also has its own Dining Room with stunning views over Fountain Court and the Firth of Clyde towards Ailsa Craig.

For enquiries and reservations please contact 0844 493 2149 or email Culzean@nts.org.uk. www.eisenhoweratculzean.com

HOLIDAYS AND CRUISES

The Trust has a wide choice of self-catering holiday accommodation all over Scotland. It ranges from luxury apartments in splendid stately homes to croft houses in the Highlands and lighthouse cottages in remote locations.

The Trust also organises a programme of imaginatively themed cruises to remote parts of Scotland and international destinations of particular cultural, historic and conservation interest.

For information on cruises and holiday properties, please contact 0844 493 2457.

If you would like to find out more about the work of Robert Adam and other notable Scottish architects, why not pay a visit to:

House of Dun

THE GEORGIAN HOUSE, Charlotte Square, Edinburgh – Charlotte Square was one of Robert Adam's last commissions.

NEWHAILES in Musselburgh, outside Edinburgh – a late seventeenth-century mansion house designed by renowned architect, James Smith.

HOUSE OF DUN, near Montrose, in Angus – an exquisite Georgian house designed and built by William Adam, father of Robert.

HADDO HOUSE, Aberdeenshire – built by William Adam for the 2nd Earl of Aberdeen.

HOLMWOOD in Glasgow – a superb example of the architecture of Alexander 'Greek' Thomson.

THE HILL HOUSE at Helensburgh – the finest of Charles Rennie Mackintosh's domestic creations.

For more information on these properties and others in the care of the National Trust for Scotland, please telephone 0844 493 2100 or log on to our website: www.nts.org.uk

Close to Culzean are a number of other attractions managed by the Trust that are well worth visiting:

Souter Johnnie's Cottage

BRODICK CASTLE, Garden and Country Park, Isle of Arran, the ancient seat of the Dukes of Hamilton. Tel: 0844 493 2152

BACHELORS' CLUB, Tarbolton, South Ayrshire, former debating club of Robert Burns and his circle. Tel: 0844 493 2146

SOUTER JOHNNIE'S COTTAGE, Kirkoswald, South Ayrshire, the home of one of Robert Burns's most famous, real-life characters. Tel: 0844 493 2147

ROBERT BURNS BIRTHPLACE MUSEUM RBBM offers you a truly unique encounter with Scotland's national poet. The museum houses the world's best collection of Burns artefacts and original works, presented along with films and installations that bring Burns's legacy bursting to life. Also part of the experience are Burns Cottage, birthplace of the bard; Alloway Auld Kirk; Brig o' Doon; and Burns Monument.

Brodick Castle

ACKNOWLEDGEMENTS
Ian Gow, Debbie Jackson, Michael Moss and Katrina Thomson.
PICTURE CREDITS
The Bridgeman Art Library; Charles Plante Fine Arts; City Art Centre: City of Edinburgh Museums and Galleries; Houses of Parliament, Westminster; Mary Evans Picture Library; National Gallery of Ireland; National Gallery of Scotland; Trustees of the 7th Marquess of Ailsa; The Trustees of National Library of Scotland; Col. Sir Bryce Knox; The Trustees of National Map Library of Scotland; By courtesy of the National Portrait Gallery, London; Philip Gale Fine Art, Wales; By courtesy of the Trustees of Sir John Soane's Museum; NTS Photo Library; Sotheby's Picture Library; The Stapleton Collection; University of Glasgow Library; Whitworth Art Gallery, The University of Manchester ; Property and Country Park photography by Mike Bolam, Angus Bremner and Gordon Riddle.

DESIGN **contagious** (0131) 553 5545   COPYWRITING Geraldine Coates (0131) 332 8787

Culzean Country Park is supported by grants from Scottish Natural Heritage. The restoration of native woodland was co-financed with National Lottery funds, distributed by the Millennium Commission, through the Millennium Forest for Scotland. In 1993 co-finance was received from the European Regional Development Fund, Historic Scotland, Scottish Natural Heritage and the National Heritage Memorial Fund, towards restoration of buildings associated and contemporary with the castle. In 1998 co-finance was received from the European Regional Development Fund; Enterprise Ayrshire; Historic Scotland; South Ayrshire Council and Scottish Natural Heritage towards the Culzean 2000 Initiative.

the National Trust for Scotland
a place for everyone

www.nts.org.uk

ISBN 0-901625-79-5

9 780901 625793